Sports Illustrated KIDS

FOR THE RECORD

THE ULTIMATE COLLECTION OF PRO BASKETBALL RECORDS

BY TYLER OMOTH

CAPSTONE PRESS
a capstone imprint

Sports Illustrated Kids For the Record is published by Capstone Press,
1710 Roe Crest Drive, North Mankato, Minnesota 56003.
www.capstonepub.com

Library of Congress Cataloging-in-Publication Data
Omoth, Tyler.
 The ultimate collection of pro basketball records / by Tyler Omoth.
   p. cm.—(Sports illustrated kids. For the record.)
 Includes bibliographical references and index.
 ISBN 978-1-4296-8653-2 (library binding)
 ISBN 978-1-4296-9430-8 (paperback)
 1. Basketball—Records—Juvenile literature. I. Title.
 GV885.45.O65 2013
 796.323'64—dc23   2012009310

Editorial Credits
Anthony Wacholtz, editor; Ted Williams, designer; Eric Gohl, media researcher;
      Jennifer Walker, production specialist

Photo Credits
Corbis: Bettmann, 30t; Getty Images: NBAE/Dale Tait, 14b, NBAE/Walter Iooss Jr., 17t;
Newscom: UPI Photo Service/Gary Harwood, 33t, UPI Photo Service/Joe Mitchell, 19b;
Shutterstock: Albo, back cover (court), Doug James, 61t, Joyce Boffert, 57t, 61b, Mike
Flippo, cover, Photo Works, 55t, 56t, 58t, 60t, R. Gino Santa Maria, back cover (ball);
Sports Illustrated: Al Tielemans, 44b, Andy Hayt, 30b, 43b, 48b, Bill Frakes, 31t, 59b, Bob
Martin, 57b, Bob Rosato, 10, 18t, 22, 35t, 39tl, 41b, 47t, Damian Strohmeyer, 31b, 37b,
41t, 46b, 49t, David E. Klutho, 35b, Heinz Kluetmeier, 11, 14t, 20b, Hy Peskin, 39b, John
Biever, 4–5, 6, 8b, 40b, John D. Hanlon, 15, 34b, 43t, John G. Zimmerman, 8t, 19t, John W.
McDonough, 3, 7b, 8m, 12b, 13t, 13b, 17b, 20t, 21b, 24t, 25t, 25b, 28b, 29t, 29b, 33b, 37t,
39tr, 42, 44t, 45t, 45b, 47b, 49b, 50, 51, 52t, 52b, 53t, 54, 55b, 60b, Manny Millan, 2m, 7t, 9t,
9b, 12t, 18b, 23t, 24b, 26b, 27t, 27b, 28t, 34t, 38, 40t, 46t, 48t, 53b, Robert Beck, 2t, 2b, 16,
26t, 56b, 58b, 59t, Simon Bruty, 23b, Walter Iooss Jr., 21t, 32

Design Elements
Shutterstock: Albo, ArtyFree, fmua, R. Gino Santa Maria, ssuaphotos

Printed in the United States of America in North Mankato, Minnesota.
042012   006682CGF12

TABLE OF CONTENTS

RECORDS OF THE COURT

*All stats are through the 2011–12 NBA regular season.

In 1984 the Utah Jazz hosted the Los Angeles Lakers in a National Basketball Association (NBA) game. More than 14,000 Lakers fans traveled to the game to witness history. Kareem Abdul-Jabbar, the Lakers' center, needed only 22 points to become the all-time leading scorer in NBA history.

The eager fans cheered as Abdul-Jabbar tied the record at the start of the fourth quarter. With eight minutes and 53 seconds left in the game, Abdul-Jabbar received the ball in the low post. He faked a move to the right before swinging back to the left and releasing his trademark sky-hook with perfect accuracy. The crowd roared to life as Kareem reached a record 31,420 points.

Ever since players from the Basketball Association of America

Kevin Durant (35) is set to break a few NBA records during his career.

and National Basketball League took to the hardwood in the 1940s, fans have flocked to arenas to watch their favorite stars compete. Buzzer-beating shots, no-look passes, and high-flying slam dunks continue to make pro basketball one of the most popular sports in America today.

Only the greatest players get the chance to play basketball at the professional level. Superstars who can pass the ball with amazing precision, shoot the ball with deadly accuracy, or continually pull down rebounds set themselves apart from the rest.

Take a look at some of the most fascinating records in the world of pro basketball. These are the players and teams who are the very best at what they do on the court. These players are the record setters.

CHAPTER 1

PLAYER RECORDS

▼ Ray Allen

Some NBA players slash through the lane and excite the crowd with amazing slam dunks. Others, such as Ray Allen, do their damage from the 3-point line. For years Reggie Miller was the king of the 3-point shot with a record 2,560 career bombs. In 2011 Ray Allen was ready to take over the crown.

On February 10, 2011, Ray Allen and the Boston Celtics tipped-off against the Los Angeles Lakers. Allen needed only two long-range shots to pass Miller's record. Early in the game Allen drilled a three to tie Miller. His next two shots were misses, but with 1:48 to go in the first quarter, he put up another attempt. Swish! With Miller watching from courtside as a television broadcaster, Ray Allen became the all-time NBA 3-point king.

The legends of basketball set themselves apart by excelling at one or more aspects of the game. These players become fan favorites who help their teams win. The players on these lists worked hard to become the greatest at what they do.

POINTS

CAREER ||||||||||||||||||||||||||||||||||||||||||||||

#	Player	Points	Teams	Years
1.	Kareem Abdul-Jabbar	38,387	Bucks/Lakers	1969–1989
2.	Karl Malone	36,928	Jazz/Lakers	1985–2004
3.	Michael Jordan	32,292	Bulls/Wizards	1984–1993, 1994–1998, 2001–2003
4.	Wilt Chamberlain	31,419	Warriors/76ers/Lakers	1959–1973
5.	Julius Erving	30,026	Squires/Nets/76ers	1971–1987
6.	Moses Malone	29,580	Stars/Spirits/Braves/Rockets/76ers/Bullets/Hawks/Bucks/Spurs	1974–1995
7.	Kobe Bryant	29,484	Lakers	1996–2012*
8.	Shaquille O'Neal	28,596	Magic/Lakers/Heat/Suns/Cavaliers/Celtics	1992–2011
9.	Dan Issel	27,482	Colonels/Nuggets	1970–1985
10.	Elvin Hayes	27,313	Rockets/Bullets	1968–1984

*Active player

RISE OF LEBRON

Current NBA great LeBron James of the Miami Heat is sure to join the career points chart someday. He ended the 2010–11 season with 17,362 points. At age 26, James was the youngest player to reach the 17,000 point mark.

▼ LeBron James

POINTS

SINGLE SEASON

1.	Wilt Chamberlain	4,029	Warriors	1961–62
2.	Wilt Chamberlain	3,586	Warriors	1962–63
3.	Michael Jordan	3,041	Bulls	1986–87
4.	Wilt Chamberlain	3,033	Warriors	1960–61
5.	Wilt Chamberlain	2,948	Warriors	1963–64
6.	Michael Jordan	2,868	Bulls	1987–88
7.	Kobe Bryant	2,832	Lakers	2005–06
8.	Bob McAdoo	2,831	Braves	1974–75
9.	Kareem Abdul-Jabbar	2,822	Bucks	1971–72
10.	Rick Barry	2,775	Warriors	1966–67

SINGLE GAME

1.	Wilt Chamberlain	100	Warriors	March 2, 1962
2.	Kobe Bryant	81	Lakers	Jan. 22, 2006
3.	Wilt Chamberlain	78	Warriors	Dec. 8, 1961
4.	Wilt Chamberlain	73	Warriors	Jan. 13, 1962
	Wilt Chamberlain	73	Warriors	Nov. 16, 1962
	David Thompson	73	Nuggets	April 9, 1978
7.	Wilt Chamberlain	72	Warriors	Nov. 3, 1962
8.	Elgin Baylor	71	Lakers	Nov. 15, 1960
	David Robinson	71	Spurs	April 24, 1994
10.	Wilt Chamberlain	70	Warriors	March 10, 1963

▲ Kobe Bryant

JENNINGS' BIG GAME

Who says experience beats youth? On November 14, 2009, Milwaukee Bucks guard Brandon Jennings lit up the scoreboard with 55 points. It happened in only his seventh NBA game, the fastest a player had reached the 50-point milestone. Amazingly, he didn't even score in the first quarter.

⬤ POINTS PER GAME

▼ Allen Iverson

CAREER ||||||||||||||||||||||||||||||||||||||||

1.	Michael Jordan	30.12	Bulls/Wizards	1984–1993, 1994–1998, 2001–2003
2.	Wilt Chamberlain	30.07	Warriors/76ers/ Lakers	1959–1973
3.	LeBron James	27.64	Cavaliers/Heat	2003–2012*
4.	Elgin Baylor	27.36	Lakers	1958–1972
5.	Jerry West	27.03	Lakers	1960–1974
6.	Allen Iverson	26.66	76ers/Nuggets/ Grizzlies	1996–2010
7.	Bob Pettit	26.36	Hawks	1954–1965
8.	Oscar Robertson	25.68	Royals/Bucks	1960–1974
9.	Kobe Bryant	25.40	Lakers	1996–2012*
10.	Dwyane Wade	25.15	Heat	2003–2012*

*Active player

SINGLE SEASON ||||||||||||||||||||||||||||||||||||||

1.	Wilt Chamberlain	50.36	Warriors	1961–62
2.	Wilt Chamberlain	44.83	Warriors	1962–63
3.	Wilt Chamberlain	38.39	Warriors	1960–61
4.	Wilt Chamberlain	37.60	Warriors	1959–60
5.	Michael Jordan	37.09	Bulls	1986–87
6.	Wilt Chamberlain	36.85	Warriors	1963–64
7.	Rick Barry	35.58	Warriors	1966–67
8.	Kobe Bryant	35.40	Lakers	2005–06
9.	Michael Jordan	34.98	Bulls	1987–88
10.	Kareem Abdul-Jabbar	34.84	Bucks	1971–72

▲ Michael Jordan

RECORD FACT When you're hot, you're hot. On March 2, 1962, Wilt Chamberlain set an amazing record with the Philadelphia Warriors. He scored 100 points in a single game! He made 36 of 63 field goal attempts against the New York Knicks. Even though he had a .511 free throw shooting percentage going into the game, he sank a remarkable 28 of 32 free throws.

FIELD GOAL PERCENTAGE

CAREER

1.	Shaquille O'Neal	58.23	Magic/Lakers/Heat/ Suns/Cavaliers/Celtics	1992–2011
2.	Artis Gilmore	58.19	Colonels/Bulls/ Spurs/Celtics	1971–1988
3.	Mark West	58.03	Mavericks/Bucks/ Cavaliers/Suns/ Pistons/Pacers/Hawks	1983–2000
4.	Tyson Chandler	57.81	Bulls/Hornets/ Bobcats/Mavericks/ Knicks	2001–2012*
5.	Dwight Howard	57.73	Magic	2004–2012*
6.	Steve Johnson	57.22	Kings/Bulls/Spurs/ Trail Blazers/ Timberwolves/ SuperSonics/Warriors	1981–1991
7.	Darryl Dawkins	57.20	76ers/Nets/Jazz/ Pistons	1975–1989
8.	James Donaldson	57.06	SuperSonics/Clippers/ Mavericks/Knicks/ Jazz	1980–1993, 1994–1995
9.	Bo Outlaw	56.73	Clippers/Magic/ Suns/Grizzlies	1993–2008
10.	Jeff Ruland	56.37	Bullets/76ers/Pistons	1981–1993

*Active player

RECORD FACT Some say basketball is a tall person's game. The saying may be true when it comes to field goal percentage. The tallest players usually play close to the basket and get a lot of short shots and slam dunks. The top 10 players on the career field goal percentage list average 6 feet 11 inches (211 centimeters). Artis Gilmore and James Donaldson are the tallest on the list, measuring 7 feet 2 inches (218 cm). At 6 feet 8 inches (203 cm), Bo Outlaw is the shortest on the list.

⛹ FIELD GOAL PERCENTAGE

▼ Artis Gilmore

SINGLE SEASON ||||||||||||||||||||||||||||||||||

1.	Wilt Chamberlain	72.70	Lakers	1972–73
2.	Wilt Chamberlain	68.26	76ers	1966–67
3.	Artis Gilmore	67.03	Bulls	1980–81
4.	Artis Gilmore	65.23	Bulls	1981–82
5.	Wilt Chamberlain	64.92	Lakers	1971–72
6.	James Donaldson	63.70	Clippers	1984–85
7.	Chris Gatling	63.28	Warriors	1994–95
8.	Steve Johnson	63.18	Spurs	1985–86
9.	Artis Gilmore	63.13	Spurs	1983–84
10.	Andris Biedrins	62.62	Warriors	2007–08

⛹ 3-POINTERS

CAREER ||||||||||||||||||||||||||||||||||||||

1.	Ray Allen	2,718	Bucks/SuperSonics/Celtics	1996–2012*
2.	Reggie Miller	2,560	Pacers	1987–2005
3.	Jason Kidd	1,874	Mavericks/Suns/Nets	1994–2012*
4.	Jason Terry	1,788	Hawks/Mavericks	1999–2012*
5.	Chauncey Billups	1,783	Celtics/Raptors/Pistons/Nuggets/Timberwolves/Knicks/Clippers	1997–2012*
6.	Peja Stojakovic	1,760	Kings/Pacers/Hornets/Raptors/Mavericks	1998–2011
7.	Dale Ellis	1,719	Mavericks/SuperSonics/Bucks/Spurs/Nuggets/Hornets	1983–2000
8.	Rashard Lewis	1,690	SuperSonics/Magic/Wizards	1998–2012*
9.	Paul Pierce	1,678	Celtics	1998–2012*
10.	Steve Nash	1,620	Suns/Mavericks	1996–2012*

*Active player

RECORD FACT It wasn't until the beginning of the 1979–80 season that the NBA added the 3-point line. The 3-point line is 23 feet 9 inches (7.2 m) at the top of the key and 22 feet (6.7 m) at the corners, making it a harder shot than a regular field goal. Chris Ford of the Boston Celtics made the first 3-pointer on October 12, 1979, against the Houston Rockets.

🏀 3-POINTERS

SINGLE SEASON ||||||||||||||||||||||||||||||||||||||||

1.	Ray Allen	269	SuperSonics	2005–06
2.	Dennis Scott	267	Magic	1995–96
3.	George McCloud	257	Mavericks	1995–96
4.	Jason Richardson	243	Bobcats	2007–08
5.	Peja Stojakovic	240	Kings	2003–04
6.	Mookie Blaylock	231	Hawks	1995–96
	Peja Stojakovic	231	Hornets	2007–08
8.	Ray Allen	229	Bucks	2001–02
	Reggie Miller	229	Pacers	1996–97
10.	Kyle Korver	226	76ers	2004–05
	Rashard Lewis	226	Magic	2007–08
	Quentin Richardson	226	Suns	2004–05

SINGLE GAME ||||||||||||||||||||||||||||||||||||||||

1.	Kobe Bryant	12	Lakers	Jan. 7, 2003
	Donyell Marshall	12	Raptors	March 13, 2005
3.	Dennis Scott	11	Magic	April 18, 1996
	J.R. Smith	11	Nuggets	April 13, 2009
5.	Ray Allen	10	Bucks	April 14, 2002
	Joe Dumars	10	Pistons	Nov. 8, 1994
	Ty Lawson	10	Nuggets	April 9, 2011
	George McCloud	10	Mavericks	Dec. 16, 1995
	Brian Shaw	10	Heat	April 8, 1993
	J.R. Smith	10	Nuggets	Dec. 23, 2009
	Peja Stojakovic	10	Hornets	Nov. 6, 2007

▲ J.R. Smith

3-POINT PERCENTAGE

▼ Stephen Curry

CAREER ||||||||||||||||||||||||||||||||||||||||||||||||||||

1.	Steve Kerr	45.40	Suns/Cavaliers/Magic/Bulls/Spurs/Trail Blazers	1988–2003
2.	Stephen Curry	44.13	Warriors	2009–2012*
3.	Hubert Davis	44.09	Knicks/Raptors/Mavericks/Wizards/Pistons/Nets	1992–2004
4.	Drazen Petrovic	43.74	Trail Blazers/Nets	1989–1993
5.	Steve Novak	43.65	Rockets/Clippers/Mavericks/Spurs/Knicks	2006–2012*
6.	Jason Kapono	43.36	Cavaliers/Bobcats/Heat/Raptors/76ers/Lakers	2003–2012*
7.	Tim Legler	43.12	Suns/Nuggets/Jazz/Mavericks/Warriors/Bullets/Wizards	1989–2000
8.	Steve Nash	42.80	Suns/Mavericks	1996–2012*
9.	Anthony Morrow	42.62	Warriors/Nets	2008–2012*
10.	B.J. Armstrong	42.50	Bulls/Warriors/Hornets/Magic	1989–2000

*Active player

SINGLE SEASON |||||||||||||||||||||||||||||||||||||||||||

1.	Kyle Korver	53.64	Jazz	2009–10
2.	Steve Kerr	52.35	Bulls	1994–95
3.	Tim Legler	52.24	Bullets	1995–96
4.	Jon Sundvold	52.17	Heat	1988–89
5.	Steve Kerr	51.48	Bulls	1995–96
6.	Jason Kapono	51.43	Heat	2006–07
7.	Detlef Schrempf	51.38	SuperSonics	1994–95
8.	Steve Kerr	50.69	Cavaliers	1989–90
9.	Craig Hodges	49.14	Bucks/Suns	1987–88
10.	Hubert Davis	49.10	Mavericks	1999–00

▲ Kyle Korver

▼ **Moses Malone**

CAREER ||||||||||||||||||||||||||||||||||||||||||||||||||

1.	Karl Malone	9,787	Jazz/Lakers	1985–2004
2.	Moses Malone	9,018	Stars/Spirits/ Braves/Rockets/ 76ers/Bullets/ Hawks/Bucks/ Spurs	1974–1995
3.	Oscar Robertson	7,694	Royals/Bucks	1960–1974
4.	Kobe Bryant	7,407	Lakers	1996–2012*
5.	Michael Jordan	7,327	Bulls/Wizards	1984–1993, 1994–1998, 2001–2003
6.	Jerry West	7,160	Lakers	1960–1974
7.	Adrian Dantley	6,832	Braves/Pacers/ Lakers/Jazz/ Pistons/ Mavericks/Bucks	1976–1991
8.	Kareem Abdul-Jabbar	6,712	Bucks/Lakers	1969–1989
	Dolph Schayes	6,712	Nationals/76ers	1949–1964
10.	Dan Issel	6,591	Colonels/ Nuggets	1970–1985

*Active player

FREE THROW STREAK ➡

Micheal Williams, a guard for the Minnesota Timberwolves, set a record for consecutive free throws. He made a record 97 straight free throws during a streak that stretched over two seasons between March and November 1993.

⚫ FREE THROWS

SINGLE SEASON

1.	Jerry West	840	Lakers	1965–66
2.	Wilt Chamberlain	835	Warriors	1961–62
3.	Michael Jordan	833	Bulls	1986–87
4.	Adrian Dantley	813	Jazz	1983–84
5.	Oscar Robertson	800	Royals	1963–64
6.	Kevin Durant	756	Thunder	2009–10
7.	Rick Barry	753	Warriors	1966–67
8.	Oscar Robertson	742	Royals	1965–66
9.	Moses Malone	737	76ers	1984–85
10.	Oscar Robertson	736	Royals	1966–67

⚫ FREE THROW ATTEMPTS

CAREER

1.	Karl Malone	13,188	Jazz/Lakers	1985–2004
2.	Moses Malone	11,864	Stars/Spirits/Braves/Rockets/76ers/Bullets/Hawks/Bucks/Spurs	1974–1995
3.	Wilt Chamberlain	11,862	Warriors/76ers/Lakers	1959–1973
4.	Shaquille O'Neal	11,252	Magic/Lakers/Heat/Suns/Cavaliers/Celtics	1992–2011
5.	Kareem Abdul-Jabbar	9,304	Bucks/Lakers	1969–1989
6.	Oscar Robertson	9,185	Royals/Bucks	1960–1974
7.	Kobe Bryant	8,842	Lakers	1996–2012*
8.	Jerry West	8,801	Lakers	1960–1974
9.	Artis Gilmore	8,790	Colonels/Bulls/Spurs/Celtics	1971–1988
10.	Michael Jordan	8,772	Bulls/Wizards	1984–1993, 1994–1998, 2001–2003

*Active player

FREE THROW ATTEMPTS

▼ Steve Nash

SINGLE SEASON				
1.	Wilt Chamberlain	1,363	Warriors	1961–62
2.	Wilt Chamberlain	1,113	Warriors	1962–63
3.	Wilt Chamberlain	1,054	Warriors	1960–61
4.	Wilt Chamberlain	1,016	Warriors	1963–64
5.	Wilt Chamberlain	991	Warriors	1959–60
6.	Jerry West	977	Lakers	1965–66
7.	Wilt Chamberlain	976	76ers	1965–66
8.	Michael Jordan	972	Bulls	1986–87
	Shaquille O'Neal	972	Lakers	2000–01
10.	Charles Barkley	951	76ers	1987–88

FREE THROW PERCENTAGE

CAREER				
1.	Mark Price	.9039	Cavaliers/Bullets/Warriors/Magic	1986–1998
2.	Steve Nash	.9035	Suns/Mavericks	1996–2012*
3.	Peja Stojakovic	.8948	Kings/Pacers/Hornets/Raptors/Mavericks	1998–2011
4.	Ray Allen	.8939	Bucks/SuperSonics/Celtics	1996–2012*
5.	Chauncey Billups	.8937	Celtics/Raptors/Nuggets/Timberwolves/Pistons/Knicks/Clippers	1997–2012*
6.	Rick Barry	.8931	Warriors/Oaks/Capitols/Rockets	1966–1980
7.	Calvin Murphy	.8916	Rockets	1970–1983
8.	Scott Skiles	.8891	Bucks/Pacers/Magic/Bullets/76ers	1986–1996
9.	Reggie Miller	.8877	Pacers	1987–2005
10.	Larry Bird	.8857	Celtics	1979–1992

*Active player

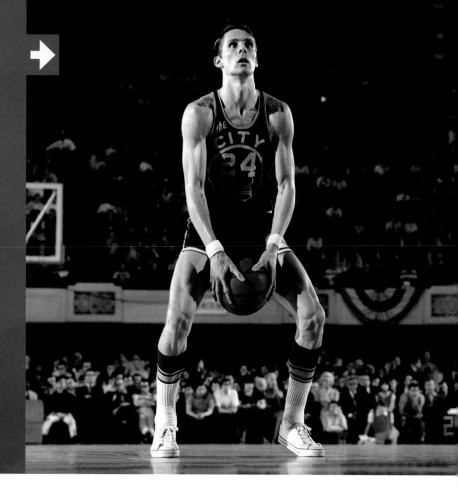

UNIQUE FREE THROWS

Rick Barry had an unusual but effective shooting style for free throws. Instead of shooting the ball from above his head like most players, he shot his free throws with a two-handed, underhand motion below his waist. He would lob the ball softly above the rim, allowing it to come down toward the basket rather than at a sharp angle. It worked. He made 5,713 free throws during his career and led the league in free throw percentage seven times.

FREE THROW PERCENTAGE

SINGLE SEASON				
1.	Jose Calderon	.9805	Raptors	2008–09
2.	Calvin Murphy	.9581	Rockets	1980–81
3.	Mahmoud Abdul-Rauf	.9563	Nuggets	1993–94
4.	Ray Allen	.9518	Celtics	2008–09
5.	Jeff Hornacek	.9500	Jazz	1999–00
6.	Mark Price	.9475	Cavaliers	1992–93
7.	Mark Price	.9474	Cavaliers	1991–92
8.	Rick Barry	.9467	Rockets	1978–79
9.	Ernie DiGregorio	.9452	Braves	1976–77
10.	Chris Mullin	.9390	Pacers	1997–98

▲ Jose Calderon

REBOUNDS

CAPEER

#	Player	Rebounds	Teams	Years
1.	Wilt Chamberlain	23,924	Warriors/76ers/Lakers	1959–1973
2.	Bill Russell	21,620	Celtics	1956–1969
3.	Moses Malone	17,834	Stars/Spirits/Braves/Rockets/76ers/Bullets/Hawks/Bucks/Spurs	1974–1995
4.	Kareem Abdul-Jabbar	17,440	Bucks/Lakers	1969–1989
5.	Artis Gilmore	16,330	Colonels/Bulls/Spurs/Celtics	1971–1988
6.	Elvin Hayes	16,279	Rockets/Bullets	1968–1984
7.	Karl Malone	14,968	Jazz/Lakers	1985–2004
8.	Robert Parish	14,715	Warriors/Celtics/Hornets/Bulls	1976–1997
9.	Nate Thurmond	14,464	Warriors/Bulls/Cavaliers	1963–1977
10.	Walt Bellamy	14,241	Packers/Zephyrs/Bullets/Knicks/Pistons/Hawks/Jazz	1961–1975

REBOUNDING REBEL

Dennis Rodman was a one-man show on the court. Heavily tattooed and sporting colorful hairdos, he often got under the skin of his opponents, officials, and sometimes even his own teammates and coaches. Rodman was a solid player who excelled at one thing: rebounding. He led the league in rebounding four times and was in the top 10 in offensive rebounds 11 times. "I'm hungrier than those other guys out there," he said. "Every rebound is a personal challenge."

▼ **Bill Russell**

SINGLE SEASON

1.	Wilt Chamberlain	2,149	Warriors	1960–61
2.	Wilt Chamberlain	2,052	Warriors	1961–62
3.	Wilt Chamberlain	1,957	76ers	1966–67
4.	Wilt Chamberlain	1,952	76ers	1967–68
5.	Wilt Chamberlain	1,946	Warriors	1962–63
6.	Wilt Chamberlain	1,943	76ers	1965–66
7.	Wilt Chamberlain	1,941	Warriors	1959–60
8.	Bill Russell	1,930	Celtics	1963–64
9.	Bill Russell	1,878	Celtics	1964–65
10.	Bill Russell	1,868	Celtics	1960–61

SINGLE GAME

1.	Charles Oakley	35	Bulls	April 22, 1988
2.	Dennis Rodman	34	Pistons	March 4, 1992
	Rony Seikaly	34	Heat	March 3, 1993
4.	Charles Barkley	33	Rockets	Nov. 2, 1996
	Kevin Willis	33	Hawks	Jan. 28, 1992
6.	Dennis Rodman	32	Pistons	Jan. 28, 1992
	Dennis Rodman	32	Spurs	Feb. 19, 1994
8.	Kevin Love	31	Timberwolves	Nov. 12, 2010
	Dikembe Mutombo	31	Nuggets	March 26, 1996
	Dennis Rodman	31	Pistons	March 14, 1992
	Kevin Willis	31	Hawks	Dec. 3, 1991

▲ **Charles Barkley**

DEFENSIVE REBOUNDS

CAREER ||||||||||||||||||||||||||||||||||||||||||||||||||||

1.	Artis Gilmore	11,514	Colonels/Bulls/Spurs/ Celtics	1971– 1988
2.	Karl Malone	11,406	Jazz/Lakers	1985– 2004
3.	Moses Malone	10,452	Stars/Spirits/Braves/ Rockets/76ers/ Bullets/Hawks/ Bucks/Spurs	1975– 1995
4.	Kevin Garnett	10,302	Timberwolves/Celtics	1996– 2012*
5.	Robert Parish	10,117	Warriors/Celtics/ Hornets/Bulls	1976– 1997
6.	Hakeem Olajuwon	9,714	Rockets/Raptors	1984– 2002
7.	Kareem Abdul-Jabbar	9,394	Bucks/Lakers	1969– 1989
8.	Tim Duncan	9,241	Spurs	1997– 2012*
9.	Shaquille O'Neal	8,890	Magic/Lakers/Heat/ Suns/Cavaliers/Celtics	1992– 2011
10.	Patrick Ewing	8,855	Knicks/SuperSonics/ Magic	1985– 2002

*Active player

JEKYLL AND HYDE

Artis Gilmore was a quiet person who turned into an aggressive player on the court. The "A-Train" led the league in rebounds, field goal percentage, and blocks his rookie year with the Kentucky Colonels in the American Basketball Association. Gilmore took home Rookie of the Year honors as well as League MVP. The Chicago Bulls selected him first when the ABA merged with the NBA in 1976.

DEFENSIVE REBOUNDS

▼ Elvin Hayes

SINGLE SEASON ||||||||||||||||||||||||||||||||||

1.	Kareem Abdul-Jabbar	1,111	Lakers	1975–76
2.	Elvin Hayes	1,109	Bullets	1973–74
3.	Spencer Haywood	1,104	Rockets	1969–70
4.	Julius Keye	1,084	Rockets	1970–71
5.	Mel Daniels	1,081	Pacers	1970–71
6.	Artis Gilmore	1,070	Colonels	1971–72
7.	Artis Gilmore	1,060	Colonels	1973–74
8.	Mel Daniels	1,039	Pacers	1969–70
9.	Artis Gilmore	1,027	Colonels	1972–73
10.	Dennis Rodman	1,007	Pistons	1991–92

SINGLE GAME ||||||||||||||||||||||||||||||||||

1.	Rony Seikaly	26	Heat	March 3, 1993
2.	Charles Barkley	25	Rockets	Nov. 2, 1996
	Shaquille O'Neal	25	Lakers	March 21, 2004
	Herb Williams	25	Pacers	Jan. 23, 1989
5.	Tim Duncan	23	Spurs	Feb. 1, 2003
	Kevin Garnett	23	Timberwolves	Dec. 5, 2003
	Kevin Garnett	23	Timberwolves	Jan. 12, 2005
	Al Jefferson	23	Timberwolves	Jan. 13, 2010
	Dikembe Mutombo	23	Nuggets	March 26, 1996
	Dennis Rodman	23	Spurs	Jan. 22, 1994

▲ Shaquille O'Neal

OFFENSIVE REBOUNDS

1.	Moses Malone	7,382	Stars/Spirits/Braves/Rockets/76ers/Bullets/Hawks/Bucks/Spurs	1974–1995
2.	Artis Gilmore	4,816	Colonels/Bulls/Spurs/Celtics	1971–1988
3.	Robert Parish	4,598	Warriors/Celtics/Hornets/Bulls	1976–1997
4.	Buck Williams	4,526	Nets/Trail Blazers/Knicks	1981–1998
5.	Dennis Rodman	4,329	Pistons/Spurs/Bulls/Lakers/Mavericks	1986–2000
6.	Charles Barkley	4,260	76ers/Suns/Rockets	1984–2000
7.	Shaquille O'Neal	4,209	Magic/Lakers/Heat/Suns/Cavaliers/Celtics	1992–2011
8.	Kevin Willis	4,132	Hawks/Heat/Warriors/Rockets/Raptors/Nuggets/Spurs/Mavericks	1984–1988, 1989–2007
9.	Hakeem Olajuwon	4,034	Rockets/Raptors	1984–2002
10.	Charles Oakley	3,924	Bulls/Knicks/Raptors/Wizards/Rockets	1985–2004

SINGLE SEASON

1.	Moses Malone	587	Rockets	1978–79
2.	Moses Malone	573	Rockets	1979–80
3.	Moses Malone	558	Rockets	1981–82
4.	Spencer Haywood	533	Rockets	1969–70
5.	Dennis Rodman	523	Pistons	1991–92
6.	Mel Daniels	502	Muskies	1967–68
7.	Artis Gilmore	478	Colonels	1973–74
8.	Julius Erving	476	Squires	1971–72
9.	Moses Malone	474	Rockets	1980–81
10.	Moses Malone	455	Stars	1974–75

▲ Kevin Willis

OFFENSIVE BOARDS

Rebounds are always good, but offensive rebounds lead to second-chance points. No player in NBA history has hit the offensive boards like Moses Malone. His career total of 7,382 offensive rebounds is more than 2,500 above the next player on the list. Malone was the first basketball player to go directly from high school to a professional league. He used his passion for offensive rebounds to build a Hall of Fame career.

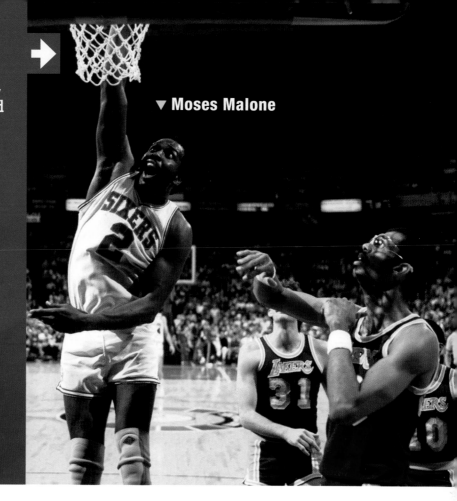

▼ **Moses Malone**

OFFENSIVE REBOUNDS

SINGLE GAME				
1.	Charles Oakley	18	Bulls	March 15, 1986
	Dennis Rodman	18	Pistons	March 4, 1992
3.	Jayson Williams	17	Nets	Oct. 31, 1997
4.	Charles Barkley	16	76ers	March 4, 1987
	Charles Barkley	16	76ers	March 20, 1987
	Andray Blatche	16	Wizards	April 1, 2011
	Terry Cummings	16	Spurs	Feb. 28, 1990
	Charles Oakley	16	Bulls	April 22, 1988
	Larry Smith	16	Warriors	March 23, 1986
	Kevin Willis	16	Hawks	Feb. 19, 1992

▲ **Andray Blatche**

ASSISTS

CAREER ||||||||||||||||||||||||||||||||||||||||||||

1.	John Stockton	15,806	Jazz	1984–2003
2.	Jason Kidd	11,842	Mavericks/Suns/Nets	1994–2012*
3.	Mark Jackson	10,334	Knicks/Clippers/ Pacers/Nuggets/ Raptors/Jazz/Rockets	1987–2004
4.	Magic Johnson	10,141	Lakers	1979–1991, 1995–1996
5.	Steve Nash	9,916	Suns/Mavericks	1996–2012*
6.	Oscar Robertson	9,887	Royals/Bucks	1960–1974
7.	Isiah Thomas	9,061	Pistons	1981–1994
8.	Gary Payton	8,966	SuperSonics/Bucks/ Lakers/Celtics/Heat	1990–2007
9.	Rod Strickland	7,987	Knicks/Spurs/Trail Blazers/Bullets/Wizards/ Heat/Timberwolves/ Magic/Raptors/Rockets	1988–2005
10.	Andre Miller	7,472	Cavaliers/Clippers/ Nuggets/76ers/ Trail Blazers	1999–2012*

*Active player

SINGLE SEASON ||||||||||||||||||||||||||||||||||||||||||||

1.	John Stockton	1,164	Jazz	1990–91
2.	John Stockton	1,134	Jazz	1989–90
3.	John Stockton	1,128	Jazz	1987–88
4.	John Stockton	1,126	Jazz	1991–92
5.	Isiah Thomas	1,123	Pistons	1984–85
6.	John Stockton	1,118	Jazz	1988–89
7.	Kevin Porter	1,099	Pistons	1978–79
8.	John Stockton	1,031	Jazz	1993–94
9.	John Stockton	1,011	Jazz	1994–95
10.	Kevin Johnson	991	Suns	1988–89

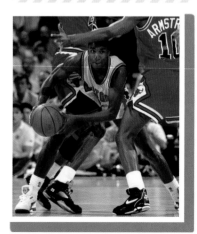

▲ Isiah Thomas

STEALS

CAREER ‖‖

1.	John Stockton	3,265	Jazz	1984–2003
2.	Jason Kidd	2,559	Mavericks/Suns/Nets	1994–2012*
3.	Michael Jordan	2,514	Bulls/Wizards	1984–1993, 1994–1998, 2001–2003
4.	Gary Payton	2,445	SuperSonics/Bucks/Lakers/Celtics/Heat	1990–2007
5.	Maurice Cheeks	2,310	76ers/Spurs/Knicks/Hawks/Nets	1978–1993
6.	Scottie Pippen	2,307	Bulls/Rockets/Trail Blazers	1987–2004
7.	Julius Erving	2,272	Squires/Nets/76ers	1971–1987
8.	Clyde Drexler	2,207	Trail Blazers/Rockets	1983–1998
9.	Hakeem Olajuwon	2,162	Rockets/Raptors	1984–2002
10.	Alvin Robertson	2,112	Spurs/Bucks/Pistons/Raptors	1984–1993, 1995–1996

*Active player

CHRIS PAUL, THE THIEF

The Los Angeles Clippers' Chris Paul is a remarkable thief on the court. In 2008, when he was with the New Orleans Hornets, Paul set the record for most consecutive games with at least one steal (106). He added two more games to his record before coming up empty against the Orlando Magic. Alvin Robertson set the previous record of 105 in 1986.

▼ Chris Paul

⬤ STEALS

	SINGLE SEASON			
1.	Don Buse	346	Pacers	1975–76
2.	Alvin Robertson	301	Spurs	1985–86
3.	Don Buse	281	Pacers	1976–77
4.	Micheal Ray Richardson	265	Knicks	1979–80
5.	John Stockton	263	Jazz	1988–89
6.	Slick Watts	261	SuperSonics	1975–76
7.	Alvin Robertson	260	Spurs	1986–87
8.	Michael Jordan	259	Bulls	1987–88
9.	Ted McClain	250	Cougars	1973–74
10.	Alvin Robertson	246	Bucks	1990–91

PICKPOCKETS

The San Antonio Spurs' Larry Kenon and New Jersey Nets' Kendall Gill hold the record for most steals in one game. Kenon collected 11 steals against the Kansas City Kings on December 26, 1976. Gill swiped the ball 11 times from the Miami Heat on April 3, 1999.

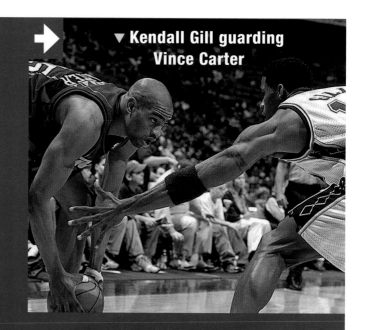

▼ Kendall Gill guarding Vince Carter

INVISIBLE THIEF

Don Buse made a career out of swiping the ball. His 346 steals with the Indiana Pacers led the ABA in 1975–76. His knack for getting turnovers didn't make him a household name, even among other players. New Orleans point-guard Pete Maravich once said that he'd "heard of him, but never seen him." Buse was a pest to Maravich during one game, stealing the ball from him four times. When asked about his lack of fame, Buse simply said, "What thief wants to be well-known?"

⬤ BLOCKS

▼ **Hakeem Olajuwon**

CAREER |||||||||||||||||||||||||||||||||||||||||||||

#				
1.	Hakeem Olajuwon	3,830	Rockets/Raptors	1984–2002
2.	Dikembe Mutombo	3,289	Nuggets/Hawks/ 76ers/Nets/ Knicks/Rockets	1991–2009
3.	Kareem Abdul-Jabbar	3,189	Bucks/Lakers	1969–1989
4.	Artis Gilmore	3,178	Colonels/Bulls/ Spurs/Celtics	1971–1988
5.	Mark Eaton	3,064	Jazz	1982–1993
6.	David Robinson	2,954	Spurs	1989–2003
7.	Patrick Ewing	2,894	Knicks/ SuperSonics/ Magic	1985–2002
8.	Shaquille O'Neal	2,732	Magic/Lakers/ Heat/Suns/ Cavaliers/Celtics	1992–2011
9.	Tree Rollins	2,542	Hawks/Cavaliers/ Pistons/Rockets/ Magic	1977–1995
10.	Tim Duncan	2,469	Spurs	1997–2012*

*Active player

BLOCK PARTY

Manute Bol holds a unique NBA record. He is the only player to have more blocks than points during his career. The 7-foot 7-inch (231 cm) center was a great shot blocker who never developed a consistent scoring game. He blocked 2,086 shots but scored only 1,599 points in his 10-year career.

BLOCKS

SINGLE SEASON

1.	Mark Eaton	456	Jazz	1984–85
2.	Artis Gilmore	422	Colonels	1971–72
3.	Manute Bol	397	Bullets	1985–86
4.	Elmore Smith	393	Lakers	1973–74
5.	Hakeem Olajuwon	376	Rockets	1989–90
6.	Mark Eaton	369	Jazz	1985–86
7.	Mark Eaton	351	Jazz	1983–84
8.	Manute Bol	345	Warriors	1988–89
9.	Tree Rollins	343	Hawks	1982–83
10.	Hakeem Olajuwon	342	Rockets	1992–93

SINGLE GAME

1.	Elmore Smith	17	Lakers	Oct. 28, 1973
2.	Manute Bol	15	Bullets	Jan. 25, 1986
	Manute Bol	15	Bullets	Feb. 26, 1987
	Shaquille O'Neal	15	Magic	Nov. 20, 1993
5.	Mark Eaton	14	Jazz	Jan. 18, 1985
	Mark Eaton	14	Jazz	Feb. 18, 1989
7.	Manute Bol	13	Warriors	Feb. 2, 1990
	Manute Bol	13	Warriors	March 21, 1989
	Shawn Bradley	13	Mavericks	April 7, 1998
	Darryl Dawkins	13	Nets	Nov. 5, 1983
	George Johnson	13	Spurs	Feb. 24, 1981
	Ralph Sampson	13	Rockets	Dec. 9, 1983

▲ Shawn Bradley

FEELIN' THE DOUBLE-DOUBLE LOVE

During the 2010–11 season, Minnesota Timberwolves forward Kevin Love put together a streak for the record books. A consistent scorer and a dominant rebounder, he put up double digits in both categories night after night. Before long crowds recognized that Love had a chance to beat Moses Malone's record of 51 consecutive double-doubles set from 1978 to 1979. Love played through knee stiffness and pain to beat the streak at 52 consecutive double-doubles on March 9, 2011. He added one more to the record before the streak ended at 53.

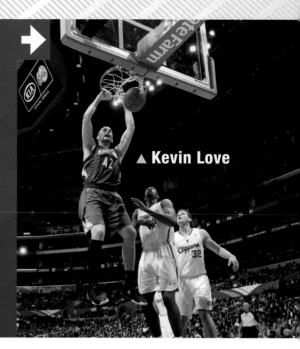

▲ Kevin Love

DOUBLE-DOUBLES

▼ Tim Duncan

CAREER

	Player		Teams	Years
1.	Karl Malone	814	Jazz/Lakers	1985–2004
2.	Tim Duncan	734	Spurs	1997–2012*
3.	Shaquille O'Neal	727	Magic/Lakers/Heat/Suns/Cavaliers/Celtics	1992–2011
4.	Kevin Garnett	719	Timberwolves/Celtics	1995–2012*
	Hakeem Olajuwon	719	Rockets/Raptors	1984–2002
6.	John Stockton	709	Jazz	1984–2003
7.	Charles Barkley	681	76ers/Suns/Rockets	1984–2000
8.	Patrick Ewing	580	Knicks/SuperSonics/Magic	1985–2002
9.	David Robinson	544	Spurs	1989–2003
10.	Jason Kidd	487	Mavericks/Suns/Nets	1994–2012*

*Active player

TRIPLE-DOUBLE MACHINE

To earn a triple-double, a player has to reach double digits in three categories. Earning one triple-double is impressive, and earning multiple triple-doubles in a season is astounding. But Oscar Robertson of the Cincinnati Royals accomplished the unthinkable during the 1961–62 season. He became the only player to average a triple-double over an entire season. He averaged 30.8 points, 12.5 rebounds, and 11.4 assists that season. He had already come close in 1960–61, averaging 30.5 points, 10.1 rebounds, and 9.7 assists. He just missed repeating the feat in 1963–64 when he averaged 9.9 rebounds.

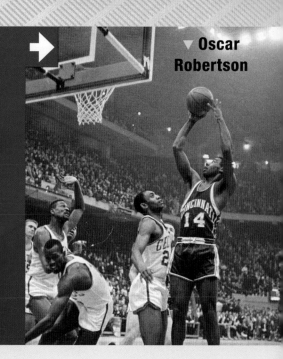
▼ Oscar Robertson

⬤ TRIPLE-DOUBLES

▼ Magic Johnson

CAREER ||||||||||||||||||||||||||||||||||||||||||

1.	Oscar Robertson	181	Royals/Bucks	1960–1974
2.	Magic Johnson	138	Lakers	1979–1991, 1995–1996
3.	Jason Kidd	107	Mavericks/Suns/Nets	1994–2012*
4.	Wilt Chamberlain	78	Warriors/76ers/Lakers	1959–1973
5.	Larry Bird	59	Celtics	1979–1992
6.	Fat Lever	43	Trail Blazers/Nuggets/Mavericks	1982–1992, 1993–1994
7.	LeBron James	32	Cavaliers/Heat	2003–2012*
8.	John Havlicek	30	Celtics	1962–1978
9.	Grant Hill	29	Pistons/Magic/Suns	1994–2003, 2004–2012*
10.	Michael Jordan	28	Bulls/Wizards	1984–1993, 1994–1998, 2001–2003

*Active player

QUADRUPLE-DOUBLES

While double-doubles are common and triple-doubles are somewhat rare in the NBA, the quadruple-double has only happened four times in NBA history. Reaching 10 or more in four categories in one game requires all-around athleticism and skill. Here are the four NBA giants who have earned quadruple-doubles.

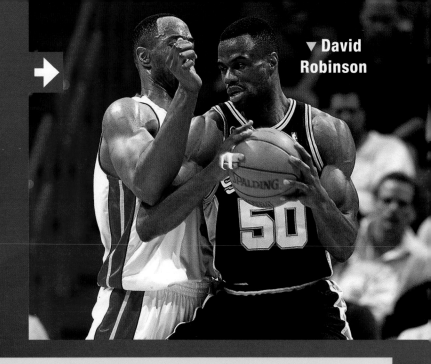

▼ David Robinson

Nate Thurmond	22 points, 13 assists, 14 rebounds, 12 blocks	**Bulls**	Oct. 18, 1974
Alvin Robertson	20 points, 10 assists, 11 rebounds, 10 steals	**Spurs**	Feb. 18, 1986
Hakeem Olajuwon	18 points, 10 assists, 16 rebounds, 11 blocks	**Rockets**	March 29, 1990
David Robinson	34 points, 10 assists, 10 rebounds, 10 blocks	**Spurs**	Feb. 17, 1994

YOUNG MVP

After the 2010–11 season, Chicago Bulls point guard Derrick Rose was named the NBA League MVP. At only 22 years old, Rose was the youngest player ever to receive the award. Averaging 25 points and 7.7 assists per game and leading the Bulls to the Eastern Conference Finals, Rose was a landslide choice for the honor.

MVP AWARDS ||||||||||||||

1.	Kareem Abdul-Jabbar	6
2.	Michael Jordan	5
	Bill Russell	5
4.	Wilt Chamberlain	4
5.	Larry Bird	3
	Julius Erving	3
	LeBron James	3*
	Magic Johnson	3
	Moses Malone	3
10.	Mel Daniels	2
	Tim Duncan	2*
	Karl Malone	2
	Steve Nash	2*
	Bob Pettit	2

▲ Larry Bird

*Active player

🏀 PERSONAL FOULS

CAREER ||||||||||||||||||||||||||||||||||||||||||||||||||||||

1.	Kareem Abdul-Jabbar	4,657	Bucks/Lakers	1969–1989
2.	Karl Malone	4,578	Jazz/Lakers	1985–2004
3.	Artis Gilmore	4,529	Colonels/Bulls/Spurs/Celtics	1971–1988
4.	Robert Parish	4,443	Warriors/Celtics/Hornets/Bulls	1976–1997
5.	Caldwell Jones	4,436	Conquistadors/Sails/Colonels/Spirits of St. Louis/76ers/Rockets/Bulls/Trail Blazers/Spurs	1973–1990
6.	Charles Oakley	4,421	Bulls/Knicks/Raptors/Wizards/Rockets	1985–2004
7.	Hakeem Olajuwon	4,383	Rockets/Raptors	1984–2002
8.	Buck Williams	4,267	Nets/Trail Blazers/Knicks	1981–1998
9.	Elvin Hayes	4,193	Rockets/Bullets	1968–1984
10.	Clifford Robinson	4,176	Trail Blazers/Suns/Pistons/Warriors/Nets	1989–2007

PERSONAL FOULS

▼ **Shawn Kemp**

SINGLE SEASON ||||||||||||||||||||||||||||||||||||||||||||		
1.	Darryl Dawkins	386	Nets	1983–84
2.	Gene Moore	382	Colonels	1969–70
3.	Darryl Dawkins	379	Nets	1982–83
4.	Steve Johnson	372	Kings	1981–82
5.	Shawn Kemp	371	Cavaliers	1999–00
6.	Gene Moore	369	Conquistadors	1972–73
7.	Bill Robinzine	367	Kings	1978–79
8.	Bill Bridges	366	Hawks	1967–68
9.	James Edwards	363	Pacers	1978–79
	Lonnie Shelton	363	Knicks	1976–77

T'D UP

Basketball can be a physical game, and players can get caught up in the heat of the moment. If a player is overly aggressive, argues a call, or makes inappropriate gestures, he can be charged with a technical foul. Rasheed Wallace holds the NBA record for most technical fouls, both for his career and in one season. Over his 15-year career, he collected 304 technical fouls. During the 2000–01 season, Wallace was T'd up 41 times.

▲ **Rasheed Wallace**

NO HARM, NO FOUL

Life in the paint can get a little rough. It's hard for big guys like centers and forwards to play their game without committing a few fouls. One of the best big men of all time, however, kept his act clean. Wilt Chamberlain, a dominating force around the rim during the 1960s and 1970s, blocked shots, ripped down rebounds, and scored with authority. What he didn't do, though, is foul. In fact, Chamberlain never fouled out of a game in his entire career.

⬤ TURNOVERS

CAREER ||||||||||||||||||||||||||||||||||||||||||||

1.	Karl Malone	4,524	Jazz/Lakers	1985–2004
2.	Moses Malone	4,264	Stars/Spirits/Braves/ Rockets/76ers/Bullets/ Hawks/Bucks/Spurs	1974–1995
3.	John Stockton	4,244	Jazz	1984–2003
4.	Julius Erving	3,940	Squires/Nets/76ers	1971–1987
5.	Jason Kidd	3,927	Mavericks/Suns/Nets	1994–2012*
6.	Artis Gilmore	3,926	Colonels/Bulls/ Spurs/Celtics	1971–1988
7.	Isiah Thomas	3,682	Pistons	1981–1994
8.	Hakeem Olajuwon	3,667	Rockets/Raptors	1984–2002
9.	Patrick Ewing	3,537	Knicks/SuperSonics/ Magic	1985–2002
10.	Magic Johnson	3,506	Lakers	1979–1991, 1995–1996

*Active player

SINGLE SEASON ||||||||||||||||||||||||||||||||||||||||||||

1.	George McGinnis	422	Pacers	1974–75
2.	George McGinnis	401	Pacers	1972–73
3.	George McGinnis	393	Pacers	1973–74
4.	Billy Cunningham	381	Cougars	1972–73
5.	Artis Gilmore	366	Bulls	1977–78
6.	Kevin Porter	360	Pistons/Nets	1977–78
	Ralph Simpson	360	Nuggets	1975–76
8.	Micheal Ray Richardson	359	Knicks	1979–80
9.	Larry Brown	356	Capitols	1969–70
	Mack Calvin	356	Floridians	1970–71

▲ Billy Cunningham

TURNOVERS

SINGLE GAME

1.	Jason Kidd	14	Suns	Nov. 17, 2000, vs. Knicks
2.	Chris Mullin	13	Warriors	March 31, 1988, vs. Jazz
3.	Gilbert Arenas	12	Wizards	Nov. 10, 2009, vs. Heat
	Dwyane Wade	12	Heat	Feb. 1, 2007, vs. Cavaliers
	Paul Pierce	12	Celtics	Nov. 8, 2006, vs. Bobcats
	Allen Iverson	12	76ers	March 8, 2005, vs. Warriors
	Jason Kidd	12	Nets	March 16, 2003, vs. 76ers
	Jason Kidd	12	Nets	Jan. 6, 2003, vs. Hawks
	Damon Stoudamire	12	Raptors	Jan. 25, 1997, vs. Bulls
	Scottie Pippen	12	Bulls	Jan. 30, 1996, vs. Rockets
	Scottie Pippen	12	Bulls	Feb. 25, 1990, vs. Nets
	Sleepy Floyd	12	Warriors	Oct. 25, 1985, vs. Nuggets

RECORD FACT Nat Hickey was the oldest player to appear in a pro basketball game. He coached the Providence Steam Rollers from the Basketball Association of America (BAA) for 29 games of the 1947–48 season. When he was 45 years and 363 days old, he put himself into a game. He scored two points off free throws, missed all six shots he took, and collected five fouls. It was the only game of his pro basketball career.

MOST TEAMS PLAYED FOR

1.	Chucky Brown	12	1989–2002
	Jim Jackson	12	1992–2006
	Tony Massenburg	12	1990–1992, 1994–2005
	Joe Smith	12	1995–2011
5.	Kevin Ollie	11	1997–2010
6.	Earl Boykins	10	1998–2008, 2009–2012*
	Mark Bryant	10	1988–2003
	Mike James	10	2001–2010, 2011–2012*
	Damon Jones	10	1998–2009
	Aaron Williams	10	1993–1995, 1996–2008

*Active player

▲ Jim Jackson

GAMES PLAYED

	Player		Teams	Years
1.	Robert Parish	1,611	Warriors/Celtics/Hornets/Bulls	1976–1997
2.	Kareem Abdul-Jabbar	1,560	Bucks/Lakers	1969–1989
3.	John Stockton	1,504	Jazz	1984–2003
4.	Karl Malone	1,476	Jazz/Lakers	1985–2004
5.	Moses Malone	1,455	Stars/Spirits/Braves/Rockets/76ers/Bullets/Hawks/Bucks/Spurs	1974–1995
6.	Kevin Willis	1,424	Hawks/Heat/Warriors/Rockets/Raptors/Nuggets/Spurs/Mavericks	1984–1988, 1989–2007
7.	Reggie Miller	1,389	Pacers	1987–2005
8.	Clifford Robinson	1,380	Trail Blazers/Suns/Pistons/Warriors/Nets	1989–2007
9.	Gary Payton	1,335	SuperSonics/Bucks/Lakers/Celtics/Heat	1990–2007
10.	Artis Gilmore	1,329	Colonels/Bulls/Spurs/Celtics	1971–1988

MINUTES PLAYED

	Player		Teams	Years
1.	Kareem Abdul-Jabbar	57,446	Bucks/Lakers	1969–1989
2.	Karl Malone	54,852	Jazz/Lakers	1985–2004
3.	Elvin Hayes	50,000	Rockets/Bullets	1968–1984
4.	Moses Malone	49,444	Stars/Spirits/Braves/Rockets/76ers/Bullets/Hawks/Bucks/Spurs	1974–1995
5.	Jason Kidd	48,068	Mavericks/Suns/Nets	1994–2012*
6.	Wilt Chamberlain	47,859	Warriors/76ers/Lakers	1959–1973
7.	John Stockton	47,764	Jazz	1984–2003
8.	Reggie Miller	47,619	Pacers	1987–2005
9.	Artis Gilmore	47,134	Colonels/Bulls/Spurs/Celtics	1971–1988
10.	Gary Payton	47,117	SuperSonics/Bucks/Lakers/Celtics/Heat	1990–2007

*Active player

COACHES

WINS ||||||||||||||||||||||||||||||||||||||||||

1.	Don Nelson	1,335	Bucks/Warriors/Knicks/Mavericks	1976–2010
2.	Lenny Wilkens	1,332	SuperSonics/Trail Blazers/Cavaliers/Hawks/Raptors/Knicks	1969–2005
3.	Larry Brown	1,327	Cougars/Nuggets/Nets/Spurs/Clippers/Pacers/76ers/Pistons/Knicks/Bobcats	1972–2011
4.	Jerry Sloan	1,221	Bulls/Jazz	1979–2011
5.	Pat Riley	1,210	Lakers/Knicks/Heat	1981–2008
6.	Phil Jackson	1,155	Bulls/Lakers	1989–2011
7.	George Karl	1,074	Cavaliers/Warriors/SuperSonics/Bucks/Nuggets	1984–2012*
8.	Rick Adelman	971	Trail Blazers/Warriors/Kings/Rockets/Timberwolves	1988–2012*
9.	Bill Fitch	944	Cavaliers/Celtics/Rockets/Nets/Clippers	1970–1998
10.	Red Auerbach	938	Capitols/Blackhawks/Celtics	1946–1966

*Active coach

CHAMPIONSHIPS ||||||||||||||||||||||||||||||||||||||||

1.	Phil Jackson	11
2.	Red Auerbach	9
3.	John Kundla	5
	Pat Riley	5
5.	Gregg Popovich	4*
6.	Many coaches tied with	2

*Active coach

▲ Phil Jackson

CHAPTER 2

TEAM RECORDS

Which team is the greatest of all time? That's a question basketball fans will debate as long as the NBA is around. The Boston Celtics of the late 1950s and 1960s rattled off an amazing 11 NBA Championships. The 1971–72 Los Angeles Lakers strung together a whopping 33-game winning streak.

No team dominated a single season like the 1995–96 Chicago Bulls. Led by Michael Jordan and Scottie Pippen, the Bulls often outplayed their opponents. Not only did they win a record 72 games, but they also defeated the Seattle SuperSonics for the NBA Championship.

Basketball is a team game, and when great players come together, legendary teams are formed. The best NBA teams earn their place in the record books.

▼ Michael Jordan

▲ Los Angeles Lakers

▲ Golden State Warriors

WINS		
1.	Los Angeles Lakers	3,125
2.	Boston Celtics	3,067
3.	Philadelphia 76ers	2,645
4.	New York Knicks	2,561
5.	Detroit Pistons	2,482
6.	Atlanta Hawks	2,460
7.	Golden State Warriors	2,352
8.	Sacramento Kings	2,346
9.	San Antonio Spurs	2,142
10.	Phoenix Suns	1,987

LOSSES		
1.	Golden State Warriors	2,794
2.	Sacramento Kings	2,695
3.	New York Knicks	2,586
4.	Detroit Pistons	2,558
5.	Atlanta Hawks	2,518
6.	Philadelphia 76ers	2,331
7.	Washington Wizards	2,279
8.	Los Angeles Clippers	2,149
9.	Boston Celtics	2,084
10.	New Jersey Nets	2,066

HIGHS AND LOWS

The Detroit Pistons and Denver Nuggets combined for the most points scored in a game with 370. In a triple overtime thriller in 1983, the Pistons scored 186 points and the Nuggets put up 184. Before the shot clock was introduced in the 1954–55 season, the Detroit Pistons and Minneapolis Lakers combined for the fewest points in a game. The two teams only managed 19 and 18 points in the low-scoring 1950 game. In 1955 the Milwaukee Hawks and Boston Celtics set a shot-clock era record for fewest total points. The Celtics' 62 and Bucks' 57 led to a record-low 119 points.

▼ Milwaukee Hawks vs. Boston Celtics

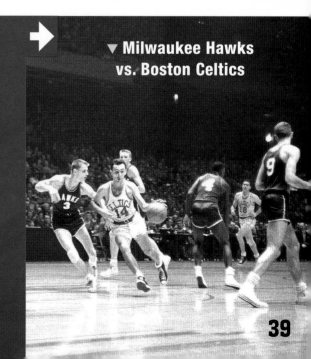

BEST SEASONS ||||||||||||||||||||||||||||||||||||||||||||

1.	Chicago Bulls	72–10	.878	1995–96
2.	Chicago Bulls	69–13	.841	1996–97
	Los Angeles Lakers	69–13	.841	1971–72
4.	Philadelphia 76ers	68–13	.840	1966–67
5.	Boston Celtics	68–14	.829	1972–73
6.	Boston Celtics	67–15	.817	1985–86
	Chicago Bulls	67–15	.817	1991–92
	Dallas Mavericks	67–15	.817	2006–07
	Los Angeles Lakers	67–15	.817	1999–00
10.	Washington Capitols	49–11	.817	1946–47

▲ Dennis Rodman
of the Chicago Bulls

RECORD FACT Two teams share the record for most wins to begin a season. The 1948–49 Washington Capitols and the 1993–94 Houston Rockets started the season with 15 straight wins.

WORST SEASONS ||||||||||||||||||||||||||||||||||||||||||||

1.	Charlotte Bobcats	7–59	.106	2011–12
2.	Philadelphia 76ers	9–73	.110	1972–73
3.	Providence Steam Rollers	6–42	.125	1947–48
4.	Dallas Mavericks	11–71	.134	1992–93
	Denver Nuggets	11–71	.134	1997–98
6.	Los Angeles Clippers	12–70	.146	1986–87
	New Jersey Nets	12–70	.146	2009–10
8.	Atlanta Hawks	13–69	.159	2004–05
	Dallas Mavericks	13–69	.159	1993–94
10.	Vancouver Grizzlies	8–42	.160	1998–99

▲ Brook Lopez of the
New Jersey Nets

LONGEST WINNING STREAKS ||||||||||||||||||||||||||

1.	Los Angeles Lakers	33	1971–72
2.	Houston Rockets	22	2007–08
3.	Milwaukee Bucks	20	1970–71
	Washington Capitols	20	1947–48, 1948–49
5.	Boston Celtics	19	2008–09
	Los Angeles Lakers	19	1999–00
7.	Boston Celtics	18	1981–82
	Chicago Bulls	18	1995–96
	New York Knicks	18	1969–70
	Philadelphia 76ers	18	1965–66, 1966–67
	Rochester Royals	18	1949–50, 1950–51

▲ Yao Ming of the
Houston Rockets

LONGEST LOSING STREAKS ||||||||||||||||||||||||||

1.	Cleveland Cavaliers	26	2010–11
2.	Cleveland Cavaliers	24	1981–82, 1982–83
3.	Charlotte Bobcats	23	2011–12*
	Denver Nuggets	23	1997–98
	Vancouver Grizzlies	23	1995–96
6.	Detroit Pistons	21	1979–80, 1980–81
7.	Dallas Mavericks	20	1993–94
	Los Angeles Clippers	20	1993–94, 1994–95
	New York Knicks	20	1984–85, 1985–86
	Philadelphia 76ers	20	1972–73

*The Charlotte Bobcats ended the 2011–12 season
with a 23-game losing streak.

▲ Antawn Jamison of
the Cleveland Cavaliers

RECORD FACT It's always good to start a season
on a winning streak. But the 2009–10 New Jersey Nets did just
the opposite. They began the season with a record 18 straight
losses. The Nets finished the season with a 12–70 record.

CHAPTER 3

PLAYOFF RECORDS

▼ Mario Chalmers (15) and Dirk Nowitzki

Bill Russell was the ultimate team player. He was a great athlete who made his teammates better by blocking shots, passing to open shooters, and playing relentless team defense. He helped the Boston Celtics rally to defeat the Los Angeles Lakers in the 1968–69 NBA Championship. With that win, Russell earned his 11th NBA Championship ring—a record that still stands.

Every NBA team starts the season with the same goal—making the playoffs and winning the NBA Finals. It's one game at a time as every team competes to become world champions. Some players have consistently risen to the occasion and dominated in the playoffs. These clutch players want the ball with the game on the line. Their efforts place them in the playoff record books.

*Playoff records are from the 1986 playoffs through June 10, 2012.

MOST NBA TITLES

#		
1.	Bill Russell	11
2.	Sam Jones	10
3.	John Havlicek	8
	Tom Heinsohn	8
	K.C. Jones	8
	Tom Sanders	8
7.	Robert Horry	7
	Frank Ramsey	7

▲ John Havlicek

MOST PLAYOFF GAMES PLAYED

#		
1.	Robert Horry	244
2.	Kareem Abdul-Jabbar	237
3.	Derek Fisher	224*
4.	Kobe Bryant	220*
5.	Shaquille O'Neal	216
6.	Scottie Pippen	208
7.	Danny Ainge	193
	Karl Malone	193
9.	Magic Johnson	190
10.	Julius Erving	189

*Active player

MOST NBA FINALS MVP AWARDS

#		
1.	Michael Jordan	6
2.	Tim Duncan	3*
	Magic Johnson	3
	Shaquille O'Neal	3
5.	Kareem Abdul-Jabbar	2
	Larry Bird	2
	Kobe Bryant	2*
	Hakeem Olajuwon	2
	Willis Reed	2

*Active player

▲ Kareem Abdul-Jabbar

PLAYOFF POINTS

CAREER ||||||||||||||||||||||||||||||||||||||||

1.	Michael Jordan	5,987
2.	Kareem Abdul-Jabbar	5,762
3.	Kobe Bryant	5,640*
4.	Shaquille O'Neal	5,250
5.	Karl Malone	4,761
6.	Julius Erving	4,580
7.	Jerry West	4,457
8.	Tim Duncan	4,233*
9.	Larry Bird	3,897
10.	John Havlicek	3,776

*Active player

SINGLE GAME ||||||||||||||||||||||||||||||||||

1.	Michael Jordan	63	Bulls	April 20, 1986
2.	Charles Barkley	56	Suns	May 4, 1994
	Michael Jordan	56	Bulls	April 29, 1992
4.	Allen Iverson	55	76ers	April 20, 2003
	Michael Jordan	55	Bulls	May 1, 1988
	Michael Jordan	55	Bulls	June 16, 1993
	Michael Jordan	55	Bulls	April 27, 1997
8.	Allen Iverson	54	76ers	May 9, 2001
	Michael Jordan	54	Bulls	May 31, 1993
10.	Allen Iverson	52	76ers	May 16, 2001

▲ Allen Iverson

RECORD FACT

Michael Jordan holds the record for most career playoff points. This feat is especially impressive because he played in only 179 playoff games. That's 58 games fewer than Kareem Abdul-Jabbar played.

PLAYOFF REBOUNDS

▼ Tim Duncan

CAREER ||||||||||||||||||||||||||||||||||||||||||||

1.	Bill Russell	4,104
2.	Wilt Chamberlain	3,913
3.	Shaquille O'Neal	2,508
4.	Kareem Abdul-Jabbar	2,481
5.	Tim Duncan	2,308*
6.	Karl Malone	2,062
7.	Wes Unseld	1,777
8.	Robert Parish	1,765
9.	Elgin Baylor	1,724
10.	Larry Bird	1,683

*Active player

SINGLE GAME |||||||||||||||||||||||||||||||||||||||

1.	Hakeem Olajuwon	26	Rockets	April 30, 1988
2.	Tim Duncan	25	Spurs	May 14, 2002
	Hakeem Olajuwon	25	Rockets	May 14, 1987
4.	Charles Barkley	24	Suns	June 5, 1993
	Tim Duncan	24	Spurs	May 23, 2003
	Dwight Howard	24	Magic	April 28, 2009
	Charles Oakley	24	Knicks	May 1, 1994
	Shaquille O'Neal	24	Lakers	June 9, 2000
	Ben Wallace	24	Pistons	April 27, 2003
	Ben Wallace	24	Pistons	May 9, 2004

▲ Ben Wallace

RECORD FACT Tim Duncan set a record and played one of his best games against the Lakers on May 14, 2002. The Spurs star not only grabbed a record-breaking 25 rebounds in that playoff contest, he stayed on the floor for 45 minutes, scored 34 points, and shot 12 of 14 from the foul line. But his feats were not enough. The Lakers beat the Spurs 93-87 on their way to becoming NBA Champions.

PLAYOFF ASSISTS

CAREER ||||||||||||||||||||||||||||||||

1.	Magic Johnson	2,346
2.	John Stockton	1,839
3.	Jason Kidd	1,239*
4.	Larry Bird	1,062
5.	Steve Nash	1,052*
6.	Scottie Pippen	1,048
7.	Kobe Bryant	1,040*
8.	Michael Jordan	1,022
9.	Dennis Johnson	1,006
10.	Isiah Thomas	987

*Active player

SINGLE GAME ||||||||||||||||||||||||||||||||

1.	John Stockton	24	Jazz	May 17, 1988
2.	Steve Nash	23	Suns	April 29, 2007
	John Stockton	23	Jazz	April 25, 1996
4.	Doc Rivers	22	Hawks	May 16, 1988
5.	Magic Johnson	21	Lakers	April 27, 1991
	Magic Johnson	21	Lakers	May 18, 1991
	John Stockton	21	Jazz	April 24, 1992
8.	Many players tied with	20		

▲ Rajon Rondo of the Celtics collected 20 assists on April 22, 2011.

PLAYOFF 3-POINTERS

▼ Chauncey Billups

CAREER ||||||||||||||||||||||||||||||||

I.	Reggie Miller	320
2.	Ray Allen	313*
3.	Kobe Bryant	292*
4.	Chauncey Billups	261*
	Robert Horry	261
6.	Derek Fisher	244*
7.	Jason Kidd	233*
8.	Manu Ginobili	222*
9.	Paul Pierce	208*
10.	Michael Finley	200
	Scottie Pippen	200

*Active player

SINGLE GAME ||||||||||||||||||||||||||||||

I.	Ray Allen	9	Celtics	April 30, 2009
	Ray Allen	9	Bucks	June 1, 2001
	Vince Carter	9	Raptors	May 11, 2001
	Rex Chapman	9	Suns	April 25, 1997
	Jason Terry	9	Mavericks	May 8, 2011
6.	Many players tied with	8		

▲ Jason Terry

RECORD FACT Robert Horry is tied for fourth on the list of career playoff 3-pointers. But he's the only player to make seven 3-pointers in a single playoff game without missing a single attempt. He accomplished the sharp-shooting feat against the Utah Jazz on May 6, 1997.

PLAYOFF STEALS

CAREER ||||||||||||||||||||||||||||||||||||||||||||||||||

1.	Scottie Pippen	395
2.	Michael Jordan	376
3.	Magic Johnson	358
4.	John Stockton	338
5.	Kobe Bryant	310*
6.	Larry Bird	296
7.	Maurice Cheeks	295
8.	Jason Kidd	290*
9.	Julius Erving	287
10.	Clyde Drexler	278

*Active player

MAGIC ON THE COURT

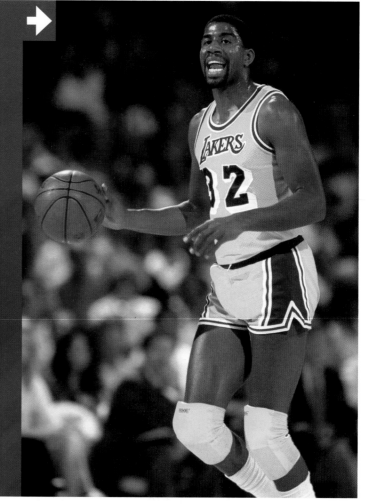

Great players raise their game when the stakes are highest. During the 1980 NBA Finals, Earvin "Magic" Johnson put it all on the line. The Lakers' center, Kareem Abdul-Jabbar, hurt his ankle in Game 5 of the series, knocking him out of the lineup. Johnson, a rookie point guard, pleaded to be put in the post in Abdul-Jabbar's place. Coach Paul Westhead gave in and let Johnson start Game 6 as the Lakers' center. What happened next is NBA history. Johnson scored 42 points, grabbed 15 rebounds, dished out 7 assists, and added 3 steals. He even played every position on the court during the game. The Lakers beat the Philadelphia 76ers, and Johnson was named Finals MVP.

CHANGED CHAMPIONSHIPS |||||||||||||||||||||||||||||||||||||

1.	Boston Celtics	17
2.	Los Angeles Lakers	16
3.	Chicago Bulls	6
4.	San Antonio Spurs	4
5.	Detroit Pistons	3
	Golden State Warriors	3
	Indiana Pacers	3
	Philadelphia 76ers	3

RECORD FACT The Boston Celtics have won more championships than any team in professional sports. During a 13-year period from 1957 to 1969, the Celtics won an amazing 11 NBA titles. No other team in North American pro sports history has matched that string of success.

YEARS IN THE PLAYOFFS |||||

1.	Los Angeles Lakers	59
2.	Boston Celtics	50
3.	Philadelphia 76ers	47
4.	New York Knicks	41
	Atlanta Hawks	41
6.	Detroit Pistons	40
	San Antonio Spurs	40
8.	Denver Nuggets	32
9.	Chicago Bulls	31
10.	Indiana Pacers	29
	Phoenix Suns	29
	Portland Trail Blazers	29
	Sacramento Kings	29

▲ Kobe Bryant of the Los Angeles Lakers

CHAPTER 4

THE ALL-STAR GAME

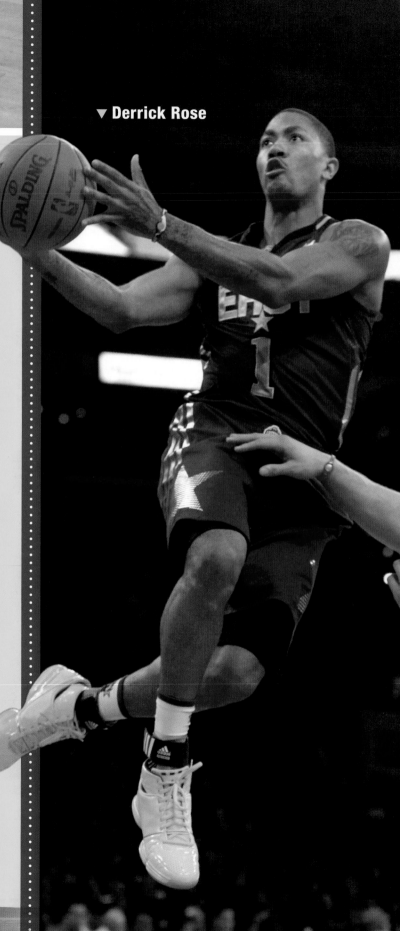

▼ Derrick Rose

In the world of professional basketball, there is more to see than regular season and playoff games. The annual NBA All-Star Game is filled with excitement as the best players in the league showcase their talents.

But more happens during the All-Star weekend than just the All-Star Game. Players get creative and show off their high-flying skills in the Slam Dunk Contest. There's something for the long-range shooters as well. The 3-point contest pits the league's best downtown shooters against one another in a shooting frenzy.

ALL-STAR STATS

GAMES PLAYED ||||||||||||||||||

1.	Kareem Abdul-Jabbar	18
2.	Shaquille O'Neal	15
3.	Four players tied with	13

POINTS (CAREER) ||||||||||||||||||

1.	Kobe Bryant	271*
2.	Michael Jordan	262
3.	Kareem Abdul-Jabbar	251

*Active player

ASSISTS (CAREER) ||||||||||||||||||

1.	Magic Johnson	127
2.	Isiah Thomas	97
3.	Bob Cousy	86

REBOUNDS (CAREER) ||||||||||||||||||

1.	Wilt Chamberlain	197
2.	Bob Pettit	178
3.	Kareem Abdul-Jabbar	149

STEALS (CAREER) ||||||||||||||||||

1.	Michael Jordan	37
2.	Kobe Bryant	35*
3.	Isiah Thomas	31

*Active player

BLOCKS (CAREER) ||||||||||||||||||

1.	Kareem Abdul-Jabbar	31
2.	Hakeem Olajuwon	23
3.	Shaquille O'Neal	19

RECORD FACT The Eastern Conference All-Stars have topped the Western Conference squad in the all-time series, 36–25.

▲ Shaquille O'Neal

MULTIPLE ALL-STAR GAME MVPS ||||||||||||||||||||||||

▼ LeBron James

1.	Kobe Bryant	4*	2002, 2007, 2009, 2011
	Bob Pettit	4	1956, 1958, 1959, 1962
3.	Michael Jordan	3	1988, 1996, 1998
	Shaquille O'Neal	3	2000, 2004, 2009
	Oscar Robertson	3	1961, 1964, 1969
6.	Bob Cousy	2	1954, 1957
	Julius Erving	2	1977, 1983
	Allen Iverson	2	2001, 2005
	LeBron James	2*	2006, 2008
	Magic Johnson	2	1990, 1992
	Karl Malone	2	1989, 1993
	Isiah Thomas	2	1984, 1986

*Active player

SHORT SLAMMER AND LOCKOUT

In 1986 Spud Webb of the Atlanta Hawks became the shortest player to win the NBA Slam Dunk Contest. At just 5 feet 6 inches (168 cm), Webb dazzled the crowd with spectacular dunks that showcased his leaping ability.

In 1998 the NBA eliminated the Slam Dunk Contest because of a lack of player interest. An NBA lockout eliminated any chance of the contest taking place in 1999. But in 2000 the Slam Dunk Contest took place again and has been a fan favorite at the All-Star Weekend ever since.

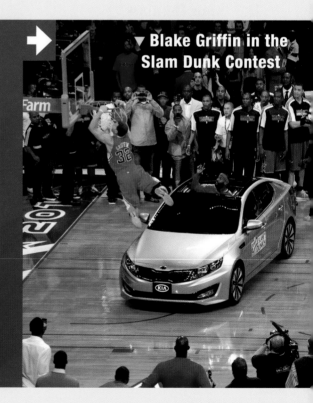

▼ Blake Griffin in the Slam Dunk Contest

MULTIPLE SLAM DUNK CONTEST WINNERS

1.	Nate Robinson	3	Knicks	2006, 2009, 2010
2.	Dominique Wilkins	2	Hawks	1985, 1990
	Michael Jordan	2	Bulls	1987, 1988
	Harold Miner	2	Heat	1993, 1995
	Jason Richardson	2	Warriors	2002, 2003

MULTIPLE 3-POINT SHOOTOUT WINNERS ||||||||||||||||

1.	Larry Bird	3	1986, 1987, 1988
	Craig Hodges	3	1990, 1991, 1992
3.	Jeff Hornacek	2	1998, 2000
	Jason Kapono	2	2007, 2008
	Mark Price	2	1993, 1994
	Peja Stojakovic	2	2002, 2003

▲ Larry Bird

RECORD FACT The 1987 NBA All-Star Game is one of the most memorable games in NBA history. After a slow start, the game picked up speed. It took overtime to settle it, with the West winning 154-149. The game set records for the most combined points (303) and free throws made (71).

CHAPTER 5

THE WNBA

▼ Sue Bird

When Tina Thompson laced up her shoes for the Los Angeles Sparks on August 8, 2010, she was preparing to jump into the record books. With about five minutes left in the third quarter of a game against the San Antonio Silver Stars, Thompson pulled up and fired a shot from 16 feet (5 m) out. Like so many times before, her aim was perfect. She passed Lisa Leslie's career record of 6,263 points to become the highest scoring player in the history of the Women's National Basketball Association (WNBA).

On April 24, 1996, the WNBA announced that it would begin play in 1997, allowing female basketball players a chance to play professionally in the U.S. The league tipped off with eight teams and has grown to 12. The WNBA has thrived behind stars such as Lisa Leslie, Rebecca Lobo, Katie Smith, and Tina Thompson. Although the league has a short history, several players have set themselves apart and earned their place in the WNBA record books.

*All WNBA stats are through the 2011 season.

⚫ POINTS

CAREER ||||||||||||||||||||||||||||||||||||||||||||

1.	Tina Thompson	6,751	Comets/Sparks	1997–2011*
2.	Lisa Leslie	6,263	Sparks	1997–2006, 2008–2009
3.	Katie Smith	6,015	Lynx/Shock/Mystics/Storm	1999–2011*
4.	Lauren Jackson	5,915	Storm	2001–2011*
5.	Diana Taurasi	5,423	Mercury	2004–2011*
6.	Tamika Catchings	5,176	Fever	2002–2011*
7.	Becky Hammon	5,090	Liberty/Silver Stars	1999–2011*
8.	Tangela Smith	5,011	Monarchs/Sting/Mercury/Fever	1998–2011*
9.	Sheryl Swoopes	4,875	Comets/Storm/Shock	1997–2000, 2002–2008, 2011*
10.	DeLisha Milton	4,863	Sparks/Mystics	1999–2011*

*Active player

SINGLE SEASON ||||||||||||||||||||||||||||||||||||||||||

1.	Diana Taurasi	860	Mercury	2006
2.	Diana Taurasi	820	Mercury	2008
3.	Seimone Augustus	769	Lynx	2007
4.	Seimone Augustus	744	Lynx	2006
5.	Lauren Jackson	739	Storm	2007
	Katie Smith	739	Lynx	2001
7.	Cappie Pondexter	729	Liberty	2010
8.	Angel McCoughtry	716	Dream	2010
9.	Angel McCoughtry	712	Dream	2011
10.	Diana Taurasi	702	Mercury	2010

▲ Seimone Augustus

● POINTS

SINGLE GAME ||||||||||||||||||||||||||||||||||||||||

1.	Lauren Jackson	47	Storm	July 24, 2007
	Diana Taurasi	47	Mercury	Aug. 10, 2006
3.	Katie Smith	46	Lynx	July 8, 2001
4.	Cynthia Cooper	44	Comets	July 25, 1997
	Betty Lennox	44	Dream	June 27, 2008
	Deanna Nolan	44	Shock	June 20, 2008
	Diana Taurasi	44	Mercury	July 14, 2010
8.	Cynthia Cooper	42	Comets	Aug. 16, 1999
9.	Lisa Leslie	41	Sparks	June 25, 2006
	Diana Taurasi	41	Mercury	July 27, 2006

MULTIPLE MVP WINNERS |||||||||||||||||||||||||||||||

1.	Lauren Jackson	3	2003, 2007, 2010
	Lisa Leslie	3	2001, 2004, 2006
	Sheryl Swoopes	3	2000, 2002, 2005
4.	Cynthia Cooper	2	1997, 1998

▲ Lauren Jackson

RECORD FACT The WNBA has had its share of powerhouse teams in its short history. The Tulsa Shock tops the chart with three championships. The Los Angeles Sparks, Phoenix Mercury, and Seattle Storm each have two titles. The Sparks and the New York Liberty have each made the playoffs a record 11 times, but the Liberty have yet to win a championship.

🏀 3-POINTERS

CANEER ||||||||||||||||||||||||||||||||||||||||||||

1.	Katie Smith	834	Lynx/Shock/Mystics/Storm	1999–2011*
2.	Becky Hammon	702	Liberty/Silver Stars	1999–2011*
3.	Diana Taurasi	663	Mercury	2004–2011*
4.	Tina Thompson	647	Comets/Sparks	1997–2011*
5.	Katie Douglas	576	Miracle/Sun/Fever	2001–2011*
6.	Sue Bird	547	Storm	2002–2011*
7.	Nicole Powell	482	Sting/Monarchs/Liberty	2004–2011*
8.	Tamika Catchings	453	Fever	2002–2011*
9.	Kara Lawson	433	Monarchs/Sun	2003–2011*
10.	Lauren Jackson	430	Storm	2001–2011*

*Active player

SINGLE SEASON ||||||||||||||||||||||||||||||||||||||||

1.	Diana Taurasi	121	Mercury	2006
2.	Diana Taurasi	95	Mercury	2007
3.	Diana Taurasi	89	Mercury	2008
4.	Katie Smith	88	Lynx	2000
5.	Katie Smith	85	Lynx	2001
6.	Diana Taurasi	81	Mercury	2011
7.	Diana Taurasi	80	Mercury	2010
8.	Allison Feaster	79	Sting	2002
	Diana Taurasi	79	Mercury	2009
10.	Shameka Christon	78	Liberty	2009
	Nicole Powell	78	Monarchs	2008
	Katie Smith	78	Lynx	2003

▲ Diana Taurasi

ASSISTS

CAREER

1.	Ticha Penicheiro	2,560	Monarchs/ Sparks	1998–2011*
2.	Sue Bird	1,780	Storm	2002–2011*
3.	Shannon Johnson	1,424	Miracle/Sun/ Silver Stars/ Shock/ Comets/Storm	1999–2009
4.	Becky Hammon	1,396	Liberty/ Silver Stars	1999–2011*
5.	Lindsay Whalen	1,347	Sun/Lynx	2004–2011*
6.	Teresa Weatherspoon	1,338	Liberty/ Sparks	1997–2004
7.	Dawn Staley	1,337	Sting/Comets	1999–2006
8.	Vickie Johnson	1,205	Liberty/ Monarchs	1997–2009
9.	Tamika Catchings	1,147	Fever	2002–2011*
10.	Katie Smith	1,124	Lynx/Shock/ Mystics/Storm	1999–2011*

*Active player

SINGLE SEASON

1.	Ticha Penicheiro	236	Monarchs	2000
2.	Ticha Penicheiro	229	Monarchs	2003
3.	Ticha Penicheiro	226	Monarchs	1999
4.	Ticha Penicheiro	224	Monarchs	1998
5.	Sue Bird	221	Storm	2003
6.	Ticha Penicheiro	220	Sparks	2010
7.	Nikki Teasley	214	Sparks	2003
8.	Nikki Teasley	207	Sparks	2004
9.	Teresa Weatherspoon	205	Liberty	1999
	Teresa Weatherspoon	205	Liberty	2000

▲ Sue Bird

🏀 REBOUNDS

CAREER

1.	Lisa Leslie	3,307	Sparks	1997–2009
2.	Taj McWilliams-Franklin	2,836	Miracle/Sun/Sparks/Mystics/Shock/Liberty/Lynx	1999–2011*
3.	Tina Thompson	2,772	Comets/Sparks	1997–2011*
4.	Yolanda Griffith	2,444	Monarchs/Storm/Fever	1999–2009
5.	Lauren Jackson	2,397	Storm	2001–2011*
6.	Tamika Catchings	2,367	Fever	2002–2011*
7.	Tangela Smith	2,318	Monarchs/Sting/Mercury/Fever	1998–2011*
8.	DeLisha Milton	2,233	Sparks/Mystics	1999–2011*
9.	Margo Dydek	2,143	Starzz/Silver Stars/Sun/Sparks	1998–2008
	Michelle Snow	2,143	Comets/Dream/Silver Stars/Sky	2002–2011*

*Active player

SINGLE SEASON

1.	Tina Charles	398	Sun	2010
2.	Tina Charles	374	Sun	2011
3.	Cheryl Ford	363	Shock	2006
4.	Yolanda Griffith	357	Monarchs	2001
5.	Sylvia Fowles	347	Sky	2011
6.	Sylvia Fowles	338	Sky	2010
7.	Lisa Leslie	336	Sparks	2004
	Natalie Williams	336	Starzz	2000
9.	Cheryl Ford	334	Shock	2003
10.	Yolanda Griffith	331	Monarchs	2000

▲ Tina Charles

⚫ STEALS

▼ DeLisha Milton

CAREER ||||||||||||||||||||||||||||||||||||||||||||||||||

1.	Tamika Catchings	775	Fever	2002–2011*
2.	Ticha Penicheiro	756	Monarchs/Sparks	1998–2011*
3.	Sheryl Swoopes	657	Comets/Storm/Shock	1997–2000, 2002–2008, 2011*
4.	Tully Bevilaqua	566	Rockers/Fire/Storm/Fever/Silver Stars	1998, 2000–2011*
5.	DeLisha Milton	550	Sparks/Mystics	1999–2011*
6.	Taj McWilliams-Franklin	546	Miracle/Sun/Sparks/Mystics/Shock/Liberty/Lynx	1999–2011*
7.	Katie Douglas	538	Miracle/Sun/Fever	2001–2011*
8.	Yolanda Griffith	529	Monarchs/Storm/Fever	1999–2009
9.	Shannon Johnson	494	Miracle/Sun/Silver Stars/Shock/Comets/Storm	1999–2009
10.	Lisa Leslie	492	Sparks	1997–2009

*Active player

SINGLE SEASON ||||||||||||||||||||||||||||||||||||||||||||||||||

1.	Teresa Weatherspoon	100	Liberty	1998
2.	Tamika Catchings	99	Fever	2009
3.	Tamika Catchings	94	Fever	2002
	Tamika Catchings	94	Fever	2006
5.	Tamika Catchings	90	Fever	2005
6.	Sheryl Swoopes	88	Comets	2002
7.	Sheryl Swoopes	87	Comets	2000
8.	Teresa Weatherspoon	85	Liberty	1997
9.	Kim Perrot	84	Comets	1998
10.	Yolanda Griffith	83	Monarchs	2000

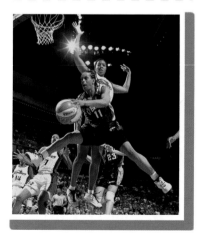

▲ Teresa Weatherspoon

CAREER ‖‖‖‖‖‖‖‖‖‖‖‖‖‖‖‖‖‖‖‖‖‖‖‖‖‖‖‖‖‖‖‖‖

1.	Margo Dydek	877	Starzz/Silver Stars/ Sun/Sparks	1998– 2008
2.	Lisa Leslie	822	Sparks	1997– 2009
3.	Lauren Jackson	579	Storm	2001– 2011*
4.	Tangela Smith	554	Monarchs/Sting/ Mercury/Fever	1998– 2011*
5.	Tammy Sutton-Brown	528	Sting/Fever	2001– 2011*
6.	Ruth Riley	481	Sol/Shock/ Silver Stars	2001– 2011*
7.	Taj McWilliams-Franklin	397	Miracle/Sun/ Sparks/Mystics/ Shock/Liberty/Lynx	1999– 2011*
8.	Michelle Snow	351	Comets/Dream/ Silver Stars/Sky	2002– 2011*
9.	Tina Thompson	328	Comets/Sparks	1997– 2011*
10.	Yolanda Griffith	323	Monarchs/ Storm/Fever	1999– 2009

*Active player

SINGLE SEASON ‖‖‖‖‖‖‖‖‖‖‖‖‖‖‖‖‖‖‖‖‖‖‖‖‖‖‖‖‖

1.	Margo Dydek	114	Starzz	1998
2.	Margo Dydek	113	Starzz	2001
3.	Margo Dydek	107	Starzz	2002
4.	Margo Dydek	100	Silver Stars	2003
5.	Lisa Leslie	98	Sparks	2004
6.	Lisa Leslie	97	Sparks	2008
7.	Margo Dydek	96	Starzz	2000
8.	Lisa Leslie	90	Sparks	2002
9.	Sylvia Fowles	88	Sky	2010
10.	Margo Dydek	85	Sun	2006

▲ **Margo Dydek**

READ MORE

Berman, Len. *The Greatest Moments in Sports.* Naperville, Ill.: Sourcebooks, 2009.

LeBoutillier, Nate. *The Best of Everything Basketball Book.* Mankato, Minn: Capstone Press, 2011.

Stewart, Mark. *The Boston Celtics.* Chicago: Norwood House Press, 2009.

Wiseman, Blaine. *Basketball.* New York: AV² by Weigl, 2011.

INTERNET SITES

FactHound offers a safe, fun way to find Internet sites related to this book. All of the sites on FactHound have been researched by our staff.

Here's all you do:

Visit *www.facthound.com*

Type in this code: **9781429686532**

INDEX